# WHERE TO EAT IN BRISTOL, BATH & AVON

AN INFORMATIVE GUIDE ... ...GHOUT
BRIS...

E... ...
Assistant ... ...
Studio co-o... ...avis
Compilation: C... ...p, Tim Stubbs

## CONTENTS
Foreword .................................................................. 3
Chef's Choice ........................................................... 4
Restaurant of the Year ............................................. 6
Win dinner for two ................................................... 7
Where to Eat in Bristol, Bath & Avon ..................... 9
Indexes ..................................................................... 58

Cover Photograph: Lucknam Park, Colerne

Published by Kingsclere Publications Ltd.,
Highfield House, 2 Highfield Avenue, Newbury, Berkshire RG14 5DS

Printed by the Warwick Printing Co Ltd, Theatre Street, Warwick CV34 4DR
and
at 112 Bermondsey Street, London SE1 3TX. Tel: 071-378 1579

Extreme care is taken to ensure the accuracy of entries, but neither the Editor nor the Publishers accept any liability for errors, omissions or other mistakes, or any consequences arising therefrom.
All prices are correct at time of going to press.

Copyright © Kingsclere Publications Ltd. 1992
All rights reserved.

ISBN 0 86204 168 6

1

# FOREWORD

(l to r) Chef Michael Womersley and General Manager Robert Carter.

# FOREWORD

by Robert Carter

It is a great pleasure to be able to introduce readers to the ninth edition of Where to Eat in Bristol, Bath & Avon, especially when it contains such a wealth of places to eat in the area.

It is wonderful to see so many different styles of cuisine in one area of Britain, ranging from New English cuisine, the follow-on from Nouvelle Cuisine, to very traditional British cooking, which some would say could not be surpassed, and then lighter, more healthy food, which is a reaction to current trends.

Lucknam Park, which is situated near the village of Colerne, has just completed its first three years of operation and, under the guidance of Head Chef Michael Womersley, is now rated as one of the best hotels/restaurants in the country. We were awarded the *Restaurant of the Year* for Wiltshire in the Good Food Guide, and Michael has also won a number of competitions, in particular the Gourmet Competition, as well as being a runner-up in the International Mouton Cadet Competition. Michael's style is in the New English school of cooking however – whilst presentation is important, it is in the taste, texture and creativity of the cooking that the strength lies.

The standards of cuisine in the area are getting higher and higher, and that does not mean just at the top end of the market. If you sample some of the more reasonable restaurants in the Guide, you get the most excellent cooking at oustanding value.

I hope you find this year's edition of the Guide useful, as I am sure, like me, you will find exactly the restaurant to eat in for whatever occasion you are planning, and I wish you a year of enjoyable dining ahead.

Robert Carter, General Manager, Lucknam Park

# CHEF'S CHOICE

In each of our regional **Where to Eat** guides, we ask an experienced chef, well-respected in the area, to prepare one of his favourite menus.

Ray and Crystal Nice have been the proprietors of Edouard's Wine Bar & Poissonnerie in Bath for just under 11 years.

After a two-year catering and hotel management course, Ray first trained at the Piccadilly Hotel, and went on to run small City of London restaurants. He worked at the famous Loose Box Wine Bar, Knightsbridge, for the Searcy Tansley Group (caterers to Her Majesty The Queen) and later set up the food operation at their newest restaurant, Charcos, in Chelsea. It was here he met Crystal, the daughter of the late Lord Russell of Liverpool and Lady Jessel. Lord Russel was the Assistant Judge Advocate General at the Nuremburg Trials and author of the famous *Scourge of the Swastika*, whilst Lady Jessel was a well-known gardening expert in Kent.

Ray and Crystal have elected to share with readers of Where to Eat a menu featuring some of their favourite holiday memories.

**STARTER**
**A Chilled Almond and Garlic Soup**

**MAIN COURSE**
**Cataplana**

*A type of Portuguese Bouillabaise, made with cubed loin of pork, live mussels, tomatoes, garlic, white wine, basil and thyme. It is served with a marinade of peppers as a side salad. This is prepared by burning the skin off the peppers under the grill, then marinating them in olive oil, black pepper and lemon juice.*

**WINE**
**Pasmados da Fonseca 1984**

*A soft, mature red from the house of Fonseca.*

**WINE**
**La Ina Sherry Wine**

**HORS D'OEUVRE**
**Courgette Fritters Served with Greek Yoghurt**

**DESSERT**
**Tarte aux Pruneaux Provençal**

*This is made with layers of puff pastry and soft, ripened prunes. Serve with crème fraîche.*

*The fritters are made with grated courgettes, chopped garlic, mint, allspice and grated parmesan.*

**WINE**
**Orange Muscat and Flora – Australian**

**WINE**
**Pino Grigio – Alto Adige 1989**

# BRISTOL, BATH & AVON
## RESTAURANT OF THE YEAR

In our continuing quest for the best eating places, we asked caterers last year to nominate their favourite restaurant in Avon, Somerset and Wiltshire. The result of this poll was that Beechfield House, near Chippenham, was named as the Restaurant of the Year. A photograph of the resulting presentation can be seen below.

This year we focused our attentions on Avon alone, and we are delighted to announce that the Where to Eat in Bristol, Bath & Avon Restaurant of the Year for 1992 is **The Forte Crest Hotel, Hambrook.**

Situated on the northern fringes of Bristol, The Pavilion Restaurant at The Forte Crest offers diners an à la carte which combines innovation without being confusingly long. The Pavilion Carvery offers 20 hors d'oeuvres at both lunch and dinner, along with the chance to create your own salad.

*Cheers! Grub up at Beechfield House during the presentation of the 1991 Where to Eat Restaurant of the Year Award. The participants (left to right) are Chris Musgrave, Editor Alison Moore and Anthony Curtis.*

# WIN A DINNER FOR TWO WITH WHERE TO EAT

We will be extending our survey for the next year's guide, and we would like you, the general public who eat out, to tell us about your favourite restaurants.

A form is provided below for you to tell us where you consider to be the best place to eat. It could be an establishment already featured in the guide, or a recommendation of your own. You can nominate a formal restaurant, a country inn, a town pub or a wine bar/bistro.

We would also like you to tell us, in 20 words or less, why you think your chosen eating place is the best.

The person who, in the opinion of the editor, gives the best reason for his/her choice, will win a dinner for two at The Forte Crest, this year's Restaurant of the Year. Everyone who submits an entry will receive a complimentary copy of the 1993 guide.

------------------------------✂------------------------------

My choice for Restaurant of the Year is
_____

at _____

This is my favourite eating place because _____
_____

Name _____

Address _____

Please send your votes to:

Restaurant of the Year
Bristol, Bath & Avon
Kingsclere Publications Ltd
Highfield House
2 Highfield Avenue
NEWBURY, Berkshire, RG14 5DS

To whet your appetite for eating out in
# BRISTOL, BATH & AVON
here is a selection of establishments
shown in colour

# REDWOOD LODGE HOTEL & COUNTRY CLUB

*Beggar Bush Lane, Failand, Bristol.*
*Tel: (0275) 393901; Fax: (0275) 392104.*

Redwood Lodge is situated just three minutes from the Clifton Suspension Bridge, in woodland bordering on the Ashton Court Estate where the International Balloon Fiesta is held. Rich colours and an original feature ceiling dominate the Garden Restaurant, which is decorated in baronial style. A typical meal here could begin with smoked fish platter, or a vegetable terrine of carrot, spinach and celeriac, sliced and accompanied by a tomato vinaigrette. Suprême of chicken with lentils, noisette of venison Baden Baden, and escalope of salmon with chives could be amongst the main courses. The Panelled Room, situated within the restaurant, is used for private dining, and gourmet dinners can easily be arranged here. Redwood Lodge also possesses a large conference centre, with 16 meeting rooms, including a 175 seat cinema.

*Just off Junction 19 of the M5, on the B3128 near the Clifton Suspension Bridge*

*Morning coffee 10am – 12noon*
*Lunch 12.30 – 2pm exc Sat*
*Afternoon tea 2.30 – 5pm*
*Dinner 7 – 9.45pm Mon – Sat; 7 – 9.30pm Sun*
*Coffee shop open 9 – 10.30am*

*À la carte £17*
*Sunday lunch £12*
*House wine £9.25 per bottle; £2.10 per glass (large)*
*Vegetarian dishes – up to 5 choices*
*Children catered for*
*A no smoking area*
*Real ales – Flowers, Boddingtons*
*Accommodation*
*Leisure/conference facilities*
*Access, Visa, Amex, Diner's Club*

**Redwood Lodge Hotel & Country Club**
Beggar Bush Lane, Failand, Bristol. Tel: (0275) 393901

Avon

# THORNBURY CASTLE

*Thornbury, near Bristol.*
*Tel: (0454) 281182*

The third Duke of Buckingham was executed before his castle at Thornbury was completed, and it fell into the hands of Henry VIII who later stayed there with Anne Boleyn. Today it is the only Tudor castle in England operating as a hotel. Over the years the castle has received many accolades for its high standard of accommodation and food. Classic English and French cuisine is served, offering dishes such as oak-smoked salmon served with a garnish of French leaves moistened with walnut oil, or fillet of Scottish beef sautéd with whole grain Pommery mustard. From the dessert menu, sample dark chocolate mousse set in a brandy snap basket on a white chocolate and Cointreau sauce, not forgetting a long-standing favourite – Thornbury Castle butterscotch pudding. To ensure that guests fully appreciate the tastes and aromas, diners are requested to refrain from smoking in the dining rooms.

*Near Bristol*

*Lunch 12noon – 2pm*
*Dinner 7 – 9.30pm Monday – Thursday; 7 – 10pm Friday and Saturday; 7 – 9pm Sunday*

*Dinner £29.50*
*Lunch £17.75*
*Sunday lunch £17.75*
*House wine £10.45 per bottle*

*Vegetarian dishes*

*No smoking in the dining rooms*

*Access, Visa, Amex*

## THORNBURY CASTLE

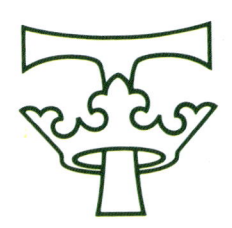

**THORNBURY NR. BRISTOL**

**TEL: 0454 281182**

## THE KITCHEN GARDEN

*Old Down House, Tockington, Bristol.*
*Tel: (0454) 413605*

Old Down House is the centre of a mixed dairy and arable farm. The Kitchen Garden Restaurant is situated in the converted stables of this Victorian estate, looking out on the walled garden where most of the fresh fruit, herbs and vegetables served in the restaurant are grown. In the summer, food is often eaten outside on the lawn or by the lily pond. Starters include home-made soup with vegetables fresh from the garden, with home-made bread rolls. Examples of main courses include local smoked trout salad, courgette pancake, home-made quiche with free range eggs or macaroni and seafood au gratin. Home-made dairy ice-cream, and brandied bread and butter pudding, are possible desserts. In addition to the food, the estate provides plenty of diversions for guests, including walks in the woods and gardens. Special functions by arrangement.

On the B4461 Thornbury to Severn Bridge road, follow signs for Old Down

Morning coffee from 9am – 12noon
Lunch 12noon – 2.30pm
Afternoon tea from 2.30 – 5pm

Closed Mondays

À la carte £11
Sunday lunch £12
House wine £6.25 per bottle; £1.25 per glass

Vegetarian dishes
Facilities for disabled guests

A no smoking area

A garden

Access, Visa

---

Victorian
Gardens
★
Licensed
Restaurant
★
Country Food
Shop
★
Gift Shop

## The Kitchen Garden
Old Down House  Tockington  BRISTOL  BS12 4PG
Telephone Thornbury (0454) 413605

Avon

*Near Winterbourne*

*Morning coffee 10am – 12noon*
*Lunch 12.30 – 2pm*
*Dinner 7 – 10pm*

*À la carte £24*
*Table d'hôte £17.50*
*Sunday lunch £12.50*
*Bar snacks from £4.50 – £10*
*House wines £7.95 per bottle*

*Vegetarian dishes such as filo basket with spinach and baby vegetables on a walnut and orange sauce*

*Children catered for*

*Facilities for disabled guests*

*Access, Visa, Amex, Diner's Club*

## THE GRANGE RESORT HOTEL

*Northwoods, Winterbourne.*
*Tel: (0454) 777333*

The Woodlands Restaurant, within The Grange Resort Hotel, provides a tranquil backcloth for any type of dining experience, be it an intimate dinner for two or a family gathering. Head Chef Richard Barker, who trained at London's Dorchester Hotel, produces dishes such as terrine of duck and pistachio nuts, served with a mango and tomato chutney parcel, or smoked salmon with an avocado and cream cheese mousse, as part of the à la carte. These could be followed by fillet of salmon baked in puff pastry with fine vegetables and fresh ginger, served on a tarragon mustard sauce, or pan-fried noisettes of lamb with tomatoes, olives, courgettes and aubergines. The meal could close with a quartet of strawberry desserts served on a strawberry coulis, or exotic fruits glazed with a Kirsch sabayon and served with a passion fruit sorbet.

The Restaurant at The Grange Resort Hotel

## THE KILN BRASSERIE

*Bristol Hilton International, Redcliffe Way, Bristol.*
*Tel: (0272) 260041*

The Kiln Brasserie, beautifully restored from an 18th Century glass kiln, provides a charming and unique setting in which to dine, with the accompaniment of a pianist most evenings. The à la carte offers a good variety of traditionally cooked food, blended with modern presentation. Starters include chilled ogen melon with a selection of sorbets and garlic prawns served on a warm salad. To follow, baked chicken and veal roulade or poached whole lemon sole with a confit of fresh seafood. The Kiln Brasserie also offers vegetarian dishes. Tempting sweets to end the meal include coupe Tahiti and pistachio diplomat. The wine list includes French, Australian and Californian wines. Private parties and conferences are welcome.

*Centre of Bristol*

*Lunch*
*Dinner*

*Restaurant closed Saturday lunchtime.*

*À la carte approx. £21.50*
*3-course carvery £16.50*
*House wine £9.95*

*Vegetarian dishes*
*Children catered for*

*Visa, Access*

### THE KILN BRASSERIE
at
**BRISTOL HILTON**

Redcliffe Way
Bristol
Tel. (0272) 260041

## LE CHATEAU WINE BAR

*32 Park Street, Bristol.*
*Tel: (0272) 268654*

The recently completed Victorian stained glass conservatory has added extra space to this ever-popular and bustling wine bar. The rest of the wine bar is a tasteful amalgamation of Edwardian and Victorian styles within a fine old Georgian building in Bristol's busy Park Street. Its interesting furnishings and comfortable atmosphere combine with its quality catering to make this a favourite venue. Amongst the features are the exquisite, antique mirror-backed bar, the Victorian snob-screen and the spiral staircase, but a myriad of old paraphernalia and decorations creates a rich ambience, enhanced by candlelight and swing music.

Menu treats include beef Stroganoff, rack of lamb, lemon sole and duck in port and orange sauce. The menu changes every day; however there are always 35 hot dishes available, as well as an array of cold temptations beneath glass. Appetisers like smoked salmon, herrings in mustard, fruits de mer and pâtés deserve to be mentioned, alongside desserts such as profiteroles and blueberry pie. For vegetarian guests there are dishes such as lasagne, cauliflower cheese and deep-fried mushrooms. Garlic bread and chips are all optional extras.

# LE CHATEAU WINE BAR

As you would expect, the wine list is extensive and comprehensive, but sensibly priced, and there are real ales on draught like Butcombe and Wadworths 6X. Hosts Bob and Denise Lewis have clearly made a success out of this 160 seater establishment, through hard work from morning (when Continental breakfast and coffee are served) to last orders for dinner at 8pm and beyond, yet no service charge is levied. Their speciality is catering for private functions (up to 50 guests) with eye-opening buffet meals.

Centrally located, Le Chateau is always busy, so it is advisable to book in order to avoid disappointment. Le Chateau also has a spirit licence.

---

Centre of Bristol,
on Park Street

Lunch 12noon – 3pm
Dinner 5.30pm – 8pm
Bar meals 12noon – 3pm;
5.30 – 8pm

No restaurant food Fri-Sun evenings

No bar food Sunday

House wine £6.25 per litre bottle; £3.30 per $^1/_2$ litre carafe; £1.40 per glass

Vegetarian dishes

Real ales – Boddingtons and Theakstons

Access, Visa

## RAJDOOT

*Central Bristol*

*Lunch 12noon – 2.15pm*
*Dinner 6.30 – 11.30pm*

*Open all week except Sunday lunchtime*

*À la carte £18*
*House wine £7.10 per bottle*

*Vegetarian dishes available*

*Fully air-conditioned*

*Access, Visa, Amex*

*83 Park Street, Bristol.*
*Tel: (0272) 268033/291242*

Established since 1966, The Rajdoot Group offer authentic North Indian cuisine in an exotic atmosphere. They were the first restaurants to serve Tandoori-style cooking in Europe. All the food is prepared by chefs who have been acclaimed as experts in North Indian cooking, and they have been specifically brought to this country to advance the cause of their native cuisine. Tandoori, cooking in a clay oven, is the Bristol Rajdoot's speciality. Guests could sample chicken shashlik or fish tikka to begin, followed by chicken narial, lamb do-piazza or makhan chicken. There are vegetarian dishes, as well as sag aloo and pilau rice to accompany. A choice from the dessert trolley, then coffee Rajdoot, could conclude.

---

83 Park Street,
Bristol, BS1 5PJ

*Rajdoot*
**Tandoori**

Telephone:
(0272) 268033/291242

For the Discriminating Gourmet, Europe's most authentic Indian Cuisine in Elegant and Exotic atmosphere.

## UNICORN HOTEL

*Prince Street, Bristol.*
*Tel: (0272) 230333; Fax: (0272) 230300*

The Unicorn, one of Bristol's leading hotels, is situated on Narrow Quay, adjoining the city centre. The hotel now boasts a Waterfront Tavern, serving real ales and a selection of popular lunchtime dishes, an up-market 80 seater restaurant, offering both table d'hôte and à la carte, and The Quayside Cafe which overlooks the harbour. Vegetarian options are available in all three eating places. A typical à la carte meal, in the restaurant, might be deep-fried Camembert with chive mayonnaise, followed by sautéd strips of veal in tomato, paprika and yoghurt, with a dessert from the trolley to conclude. Alternatively, try avocado and mushroom in a Stilton dressing, then baked fillet of sea bass with Pernod. The set menus offer value for money, and present a choice of three starters and main courses, then sweets or cheese and biscuits.

*On Narrow Quay*

*Morning coffee 7am – 12noon*
*Lunch 12.30 – 2pm*
*Afternoon tea 2 – 6pm*
*Dinner 6.30 – 10pm (Mon-Thurs), 7 – 10pm (Fri – Sun)*
*Bar meals 12 noon – 2pm*

*Closed for lunch on Saturday*
*Quayside Cafe open all day every day*

*À la carte £17*
*Table d'hôte £14*
*Sunday lunch £12.50*
*Bar meals from £2.50*
*House wine £8.50 per bottle; £1.30 per glass*

*Vegetarian dishes*
*Facilities for the diabled*
*A no smoking area*

*Access, Visa, American Express*

**UNICORN HOTEL** — PRINCE STREET, BRISTOL — TEL: 0272 230333 FAX: 0272 230300

## THE BRISTOL MOAT HOUSE HOTEL

*Victoria Street, Bristol.*
*Tel: (0272) 255010*

|  |
|---|
| 1 mile from M32, 200 yards from Temple Meads Railway Station |
| Morning coffee 8am – 12noon
Lunch 12noon – 2pm
Bar meals 11am – 2pm; 7 – 10pm
Dinner 7 – 10pm |
| À la carte £31
Table d'hôte £19.50
Sunday lunch £12.95
Bar meals from £2.50
House wine £9.95 per bottle; £1.95 per glass |
| Regular vegetarian dishes
Children catered for |
| Facilities for disabled guests
A no smoking area |
| Access, Visa, Amex, Diner's Club |

Classic décor and good guest facilities are highlights of this modern hotel. Within its walls you will find the Spires Bar and Restaurant, a mini gym, sunbeds, as well as conference and banqueting facilities for 200 guests. A resident pianist entertains guests most evenings in the bar and restaurant named after the church spires of Bristol. The hospitality and service of the restaurant staff is the backcloth for international cuisine, which could start with ravioli of salmon, monkfish and lobster laced with garden herbs. Roulade of chicken and tarragon with a Roquefort sauce, or filo pastry filled with wild mushrooms and surrounded by a creamy sherry sauce are possible main courses. Crème brûlée topped with raspberries and a sugar cage could conclude. The extensive wine list features over 80 bins. Many special events are planned for the coming year.

SPIRES RESTAURANT at
## THE BRISTOL MOAT HOUSE HOTEL
Victoria Street, Bristol.    Tel: (0272) 255010

*Centre of Bristol*

*Morning coffee 9am – 12noon*
*Lunch 12noon – 2.15pm*
*Afternoon tea 2.15 – 6pm*
*Dinner 7 – 10.30pm*

*Closed Saturday lunchtime*

*À la carte £25*
*Table d'hôte dinner £16*
*Sunday lunch £10.95*
*House wine £8.50 per bottle; £1.65 per glass*

*Vegetarian meals*
*Children's menu*
*Facilities for disabled guests*

*A no smoking area*

*Access, Visa, Amex, Diner's Club*

## THE BRASS NAILS AT THE GRAND HOTEL

*Broad Street, Bristol.*
*Tel: (0272) 291645; Fax: (0272) 227619*

The Brass Nails Restaurant welcomes guests into a setting of mirrored ceilings and walls panelled with Japanese oak. The restaurant has won a Heart Beat award for providing healthy dishes. The à la carte selection tempts diners to sample pàté with Norfolk chutney, deep-fried mushrooms stuffed with Stilton cheese and apple, or escargots sautéd with sundried tomatoes and garlic. The soup course has interesting options such as truffle soup en croûte or a rich home-made shellfish soup. Steamed mussels are always featured when in season. The traditional main courses of the finest meats and fish are roast rack of lamb with Dijon mustard, fillet steak au poivre or Dover sole Albert, veal chop with walnut butter and white wine or a hearty game pie. The vegetarian menu offers a fresh tomato salad with imported hand-made mozzarella cheese followed by a vegetable casserole of eggplant and tomato sauce. There is a special children's menu.

*at*

## The Grand Hotel
## Broad Street
## Bristol

Tel. (0272) 291645

## THE CLIFFE HOTEL AND COTERIE RESTAURANT

*Limpley Stoke, near Bath.*
*Tel: (0225) 723226*

Canadians Bill and Tracey Mallinson are the owners of the old English country house. They came to Avon with wide experience in the hotel trade, and the high standards they have set are reflected in the menu, which draws on influences from French and traditional English cooking. Strips of beef and pimentoes, marinated in a garlic vinaigrette, is one possible starter. It could be followed by pan-fried fillet of pork with oriental vegetables and fried rice. Alternatively, sample carrot, caraway and orange soup, then veal Stroganoff with oyster mushrooms and shallots. The restaurant is set against a tranquil background, featuring panoramic views over the Avon Valley. Guests in need of relaxation might indulge themselves in a special Romantic Break.

*Overlooking the Avon Valley*

*Morning coffee*
*Lunch*
*Afternoon tea*
*Dinner*
*Bar meals*

*Table d'hôte £17 – £21.50*
*Sunday lunch £10.95 – £13.50*
*Bar snacks from £2.95 – £6.95*
*House wine £10.05 per bottle; £5.80 per half bottle*

*Vegetarian dishes*

*Children catered for*

*Access, Visa*

### THE CLIFFE HOTEL
LIMPLEY STOKE. Nr BATH
TELEPHONE (0225) 723226

## THE RIVERSIDE RESTAURANT AT SALTFORD MARINA

*The Shallows, Saltford, near Bath.*
*Tel: (0225) 873862*

As its name suggests, The Riverside Restaurant occupies a lovely position overlooking the River Avon at Kelston Lock. The restaurant offers an à la carte, supplemented by chef's specials which are also available at lunchtimes, together with a range of cooked meals and bar food. A typical meal could feature Riverside nibbles (cheesey chunks, breadcrumbed and deep-fried, served with a selection of dips), Caribbean chicken (chicken suprême sautéd with pineapple, flamed with light rum and finished with a purée of banana and cream) or vegetarian envelope (home-made ratatouille within a filo pastry envelope). The carvery Sunday lunch makes families welcome, and there is a choice of roast joints, along with vegetarian dishes, starters and a dessert trolley. The Boaters Bar and Function Rooms are available for private parties.

At Saltford Marina, just off the A4 Bath-Bristol road
Morning coffee 10am – 12noon, Lunch 12noon – 2.30pm, Afternoon tea Summer only, Dinner 7 – 10.30pm, Bar meals 12noon – 2.30pm; 6.30 – 9.30pm
À la carte £12.50
Sunday lunch £11.95
Bar meals from £2.95
House wine £7 per bottle; £1.20 per glass
Access, Visa, Amex, Diner's Club

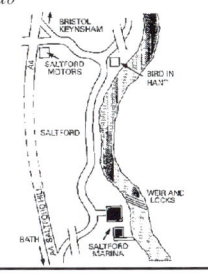

The elegant Restaurant and (inset) a view from the River Avon of the **RIVERSIDE RESTAURANT** at Saltford Marina The Shallows Saltford, Bath Tel: (0225) 873862

## THE CANARY SHOP AND RESTAURANT

*3 Queen Street, Bath.*
*Tel: (0225) 424846*

The Canary has won the Tea Council's Top Tea Room of the Year Award for its selection of 40 fine teas. Choosing your tea, however, is only part of the pleasure of a visit to this homely, pretty restaurant, which has been firmly established for well over 20 years in one of Bath's earliest Georgian cobbled streets. Continental and English breakfasts are offered, as well as lunch and supper. The international cuisine offers tartlets filled with salmon, blue cheese, pine kernels and mushrooms, or baked sardines stuffed with bread crumbs, pine kernels, chopped anchovy, herbs and orange juice. Main courses include halibut steak served on a bed of aromatic vegetables, chicken breast with herbs, courgettes, aubergines and peppers, and duck breast with brandied apple sauce. Try summer pudding for dessert. Classic and organic wines add to the enjoyment.

*Centre of Bath*

*Morning coffee from 9am*
*Lunch*
*Afternoon tea*
*Dinner through to 8pm; 9pm in summer-time*

*Closed Christmas Day and Boxing Day*

*À la carte £6.50 – £10.50*
*House wine £7.50 per bottle; £1.50 per glass*

*Vegetarian dishes*

*Children's portions*

*A no smoking area*

*Access, Visa*

*open for Breakfast, Coffee, Luncheon, Afternoon Tea, Early Supper*

Egon Ronay
Listed
Les Routiers
Recommended

**3 QUEEN STREET**
**BATH**
**0225 424846**

Tea Council
Award
for Excellence,
1989

## NUMBER 1 RESTAURANT AT THE COMPASS HOTEL

*North Parade, Bath.*
*Tel: (0225) 461603; Fax: (0225) 447758*

The Compass Hotel is situated in the heart of Bath, close to the Abbey, Roman Baths and Pump Room. It reopened in 1990, following extensive refurbishment. The décor in the restaurant is traditional Wedgwood Blue, in keeping with the fashion of the 1740's when the hotel was first built. For dinner, guests can choose from a three course table d'hôte, or an à la carte selection. Try beef sate – skewered, marinated strips of beef fillet in curry powder and coriander, served with peanut and cucumber relish – as a starter. Main courses include the Bath rib roast (rack of lamb cooked with fresh rosemary), and three fillets of beef, pork and lamb in a red wine sauce with mushrooms and herbs. There are also vegetarian dishes. A brandy snap basket filled with ice-cream and fruit, and a chocolate and Cointreau bavarois, are examples from the sweet menu.

*Bath city centre*

*Dinner 7.15 – 9.15pm*
*Bar meals 12noon – 2.15pm*

*À la carte £18.50*
*Table d'hôte £12.95*
*Bar meals from £2*
*House wine £7.50 per bottle;*
*£1.50 per glass*

*Regular vegetarian dishes*

*Children catered for*

*A no smoking area*

*Accommodation available*

*Access, Visa, Amex, Diner's Club*

No.1 RESTAURANT AT THE COMPASS HOTEL, NORTH PARADE, BATH
TELEPHONE: (0225) 461603

## SALLY LUNN'S REFRESHMENT HOUSE

*4 North Parade Passage, Bath.*
*Tel: (0225) 461634*

Everyone knows the Sally Lunn brioche, but now guests can sample the atmosphere of this very old eating house in an evening. The set menus offer good value for money, with vegetables cooked individually to order for each customer. The salmon and the venison are reputed to be good. Owners Mike and Angela have an innovative approach to running a restaurant, and this is reflected in the pricing structure for the comprehensive wine list. Rather than taking the traditional route of a set percentage mark-up on the wholesale price of a particular bottle, the policy at Sally Lunn's is that all bottles have exactly the same amount added to their wholesale price. Hence guests will find Chablis at under £11 and New Zealand Sauvignon at less than £8.50. During the day Sally Lunn's is frequented by devotees of the famous brioche. The Sally Lunn dates from 1680 when the lady herself came to the building as a French refugee.

---

*Centre of Bath, just off Abbey Green*

*Coffee, teas and light meals throughout the day*

*Dinner from 6pm (except Monday)*

*Closed Christmas, Boxing and New Year's Day*

*À la carte £7 – £14*
*Set meals from £9*
*Wines from £6.30 per bottle; £1.30 per glass*

*Vegetarian dishes*

*A no smoking restaurant*

*Access, Visa*

---

# SALLY LUNN'S REFRESHMENT HOUSE
## NORTH PARADE PASSAGE, BATH AVON BA1 1NX Tel: (0225) 461634

by very modestly priced fine wines. Reservations are advised.

SALLY LUNN came as a young girl, to this house in 1680 and made her wonderful large light brioche breads that today are known by her name.

Relax in the homely atmosphere of the OLDEST HOUSE in Bath. Enjoy a delicious SALLY LUNN, one of the City's renowned delicacies. Baked on the premises to the original secret recipe.

Light meals and snacks based on the famous SALLY LUNN are served all day, every day, with fine teas, coffees, alcoholic and soft drinks.

Dinner by Candlelight each evening except Mondays. Served in this delightful atmosphere accompanied

## THE THEATRE VAULTS RESTAURANT

*The Theatre Royal, Bath.*
*Tel: (0225) 442265*

I n the cool and relaxed setting of the original vaults of the beautiful Georgian Theatre Royal, the Theatre Vaults is an unusual venue in which to enjoy cooking in the French style. The menu, changed daily, is based on fresh produce and there is an extensive wine list of over 30 well-chosen vintages. At lunchtime there may be a light dish like croque madame or chicken liver crêpe. Steaks, chicken à la king or pork cassoulet could be among the entrées. Rack of lamb and spinach lasagne are popular with evening diners. Tables can be booked before or after the show, or independently of the theatre. Access to the Theatre Vaults is through the theatre foyer from St John Place.

*Centre of Bath*

*Morning coffee*
*Lunch*
*Afternoon tea*
*Pre-show supper*
*After-show dinner*

*Restaurant closed Sunday*

*À la carte (supper) £7.50*
*À la carte (dinner) £12*
*Lunch £5*
*House wine £6 per bottle*

*Vegetarian dishes*

*Access, Visa*

# THE THEATRE VAULTS
## RESTAURANT

THE THEATRE ROYAL, BATH.          TEL. (0225) 442265

## THE ROYAL CRESCENT HOTEL

*16 Royal Crescent, Bath.*
*Tel: (0225) 319090; Fax: (0225) 339401.*

Bath's famous Royal Crescent is home to the elegant Royal Crescent Hotel, and The Dower House Restaurant mixes classic décor, soft fabrics and pastel colours with fine paintings, antique furniture and real fires. The Dower House Lounge is the setting for pre- and post-dinner drinks, as well as for coffee and petits fours. Situated at the bottom of the hotel's walled garden, The Dower House was once the home of the Lady Dowager, and the menu here offers the best of English cuisine. Marinated winglets served with a pithivier of liver, or lasagne of langoustines in a soft herb butter, are possible starters. Crown of lamb bound in a light mousseline with a spaghetti of vegetables and lentils du puy is a possible main course. An alternative could be meunière of red mullet on an olive pimento butter scented with thyme, or lasagne of leek and courgettes with wood mushrooms glazed in a mustard cream sauce.

*Centre two houses of the Royal Crescent*

Coffee and tea available throughout the day
Lunch 12.30 – 2pm
Afternoon tea 3.30 – 5.30pm
Dinner 7 – 9.30pm

*Table d'hôte dinner £28 (3 courses inc coffee, petits fours and VAT)*
*Lunch (3 courses) £21*
*Lunch (2 courses) £17*
*House wines from £15 per bottle*

*Vegetarian menu*

*Access, Visa, Amex, Diner's Club*

**THE ROYAL CRESCENT HOTEL.** TEL: BATH (0225) 319090

## LANSDOWN GROVE HOTEL
*Lansdown Road, Bath.*
*Tel: (0225) 315891*

**T**he Lansdown Grove is an elegant hotel overlooking the beautiful city of Bath. Visitors find a gracious welcome in the reception area with its fine old fireplace and comfortable armchairs. In the well-appointed restaurant small and larger tables, all spread with beige linen and fresh flowers, are arranged to create a sociable informality, wicker-backed chairs adding to the comfort. Interesting starters include a warm salad of smoked chicken and asparagus or, for vegetarians, spinach and mozzarella ravioli on a basil and tomato coulis. To follow guests could choose fricassée of Cornish scallops or duck breast with apple and Calvados sauce. Many different desserts are offered, or there is a well-stocked cheeseboard before coffee.

*Centre of Bath*

*Morning coffee*
*Lunch*
*Dinner*

*À la carte from £20*
*Table d'hôte from £16.50*
*House wine from £8.30 per bottle*

*Vegetarian dishes*

*Access, Visa, Amex*

LANSDOWN GROVE HOTEL, Lansdown Road, Bath.   TEL: (0225) 315891

*Just off the A4, 1 1/2 miles from the centre of Bath*

*Lunch (booking essential)
Dinner
Bar meals
Traditional Sunday lunch*

*À la carte from £12
Table d'hôte from £9.95
Sunday lunch from £8.75*

*Vegetarian meals*

*A special children's menu*

*Access, Visa*

## THE WATER WHEEL RESTAURANT

*Old Mill Hotel, Tollbridge Road, Bath.
Tel: (0225) 858476; Fax: (0225) 852600*

Situated just one and a half miles from the centre of Bath, The Old Mill enjoys an idyllic setting astride the River Avon, overlooking the weir frequented by ducks and swans. The lawns, which sweep down to the water, are floodlit in the evening. The Old Mill offers several venues for dining, with a number of different menus. Bar meals can be had in the new Mill Room, and bar or more formal meals can be taken in the revolving Water Wheel Restaurant, complete with rotating base (details of this can be found on the inside of the back cover). A typical meal in the Water Wheel could be tuna fish salad, followed by noisettes of lamb with pear in a red wine and mint sauce. A good venue for wedding receptions, private parties and business conferences, The Old Mill also offers piano and dancing evenings.

# OLD MILL HOTEL

Tollbridge Road, Bath BA1 7DE. Tel: (0225) 852344

## LUCKNAM PARK

*Colerne.*
*Tel: (0225) 742777; Fax: (0225) 743536*

Just six miles from Bath, Lucknam Park is set in beautiful countryside on the southern edge of the Cotswolds. A magnificent country house hotel, it has 42 bedrooms, all of which are decorated with antiques and paintings from the late Georgian and early Victorian periods. The Head Chef, Michael Womersley, spent two years at Le Manoir aux Quat' Saisons prior to coming to Lucknam, and the cuisine he prepares is modern English. Consommé of mussels and clams with their shells farcie, or home-made tagliatelli with a pesto sauce and cherry tomatoes, could precede grilled salmis of squab pigeon with a parsley sauce and a casserole of its legs. A hazelnut box with cherries, set on a Kirsh mocha sauce, could conclude. Within the walled gardens of the hotel, there is a leisure spa, including an indoor heated swimming pool, and there are five meeting rooms for conferences.

*Six miles from Bath*

*Morning coffee when required*

*Lunch 12.30 – 2pm;*
*2.30pm Sun*
*Afternoon tea 3.30 –*
*5.30pm*
*Dinner 7.30 – 9.30pm*

*À la carte £35*
*Sunday lunch £19.50*
*House wine £15 per bottle*

*Vegetarian dishes on request*
*Children's meals on request*

*Facilities for disabled guests*
*Accommodation*

*Leisure/conference facilities*

*Access, Visa, Amex, Diner's Club, JTB, Eurocard, Mastercard*

## LUCKNAM PARK
### COLERNE, NR BATH
TELEPHONE (0225) 742777

*A member of small luxury hotels of the World*

## REDWOOD LODGE HOTEL & COUNTRY CLUB

*Beggar Bush Lane, Failand, Bristol.*
*Tel: (0275) 393901; Fax: (0275) 392104*

J ust three minutes from the Clifton Suspension Bridge, Redwood Lodge is set within woodland bordering Ashton Court. The baronial-style Garden Restaurant could yield a vegetable terrine, then suprême of chicken with lentils. Please see page 9 for more information.

## THORNBURY CASTLE

*Thornbury, near Bristol.*
*Tel: (0454) 281182*

T he third Duke of Buckingham was executed before his castle at Thornbury was completed. Today it is the only Tudor castle in England operating as a hotel, and has won many awards for the standard of its accommodation and food. Classic English and French dishes, such as oak-smoked salmon with a garnish of French leaves, are found on the menu. For more information, please see page 10.

## THE KITCHEN GARDEN

*Old Down House, Tockington, Bristol.*
*Tel: (0454) 413605*

O ld Down House is the centre of a mixed dairy and arable farm, and The Kitchen Garden restaurant is situated in the converted stables, overlooking the walled garden where many of the herbs and vegetables used in the cooking are grown. A typical meal could feature home-made soup, then seafood au gratin. Please see page 11 for more information.

*Kingsclere Publications produces a varied list of publications in the* **Where to Eat** *series which cover areas as far apart as Scotland, The Channel Isles and Ireland.*

## THE BOWL INN & RESTAURANT
Church Road, Lower Almondsbury.
Tel: (0454) 612757/613717

Nestling on the south eastern edge of the Severn Vale, within sight of the estuary, yet only 5 minutes from the M4/M5 Almondsbury Interchange, The Bowl Inn is a picturesque whitewashed stone building, dating from the 17th century. The Bowl provides a wide range of bar snacks, or alternatively guests may eat in the intimate restaurant, where the extensive menus are both traditional and Continental.

*Adjacent to the Church of St Mary*

*Morning coffee*
*Lunch*
*Dinner*
*Bar meals*
*Restaurant closed Sunday evenings and Christmas Day*

*À la carte £14*
*Business lunch £6.95*
*Traditional Sunday lunch (adults) £6.95;*
*(children under 12) £4.25*
*House wine £6.25 per bottle*

*Vegetarian dishes*
*Children catered for*
*Facilities for the disabled (the pub is on one level with no steps)*

*Accommodation available*

*Access, Visa, Amex, Diner's Club*

**THE BOWL INN & RESTAURANT**

*Known for exquisite cuisine and fine wines in a friendly relaxed atmosphere.*

*Next to St. Mary's Church, Lower Almondsbury.*
*Tel: 0454 612757/ 613717*

## THE GRANGE RESORT HOTEL
Northwoods, Winterbourne.
Tel: (0454) 777333

The Woodlands Restaurant at The Grange Resort offers a tranquil setting for any type of dining out occasion. Terrine of duck with pistachio nuts could precede fillet of salmon baked in puff pastry. Exotic fruits glazed with Kirsch sabayon could conclude. Please see page 12 for more information.

*Thanks to the vital support of advertisers and readers alike, more comprehensive guides are being prepared. Each guide is freshly researched, revised and updated each year!*

Avon

# The Wheatsheaf
## WINTERBOURNE

*Winterbourne High Street*

Morning coffee
Lunch
Dinner

À la carte £12
Carvery luncheon £5 – £9.75
Bar snacks from £2.50 – £4.50
House wine £8.95 per litre

Good selection of vegetarian dishes, including vegetarian specials
Facilities for the disabled

Access, Visa, Amex, Diner's Club

*High Street, Winterbourne.*
*Tel: (0454) 773758*

At The Wheatsheaf Inn, in the middle of Winterbourne's High Street, you will find an intriguing collection of agricultural and rural artefacts, old photographs and other memorabilia. Only fresh produce and quality ingredients enter the kitchen. Main courses include a selection of steaks, dishes such as beef Stroganoff and breast of chicken in leek and Stilton sauce, and a range of light meals, including tortellini carbonara. Starters are popular and varied, offering baked garlic mushrooms and seafood provençale amongst others. The Wheatsheaf has become renowned for its lunchtime carvery, which has proved very popular with the business fraternity, not least because of the prompt service and value for money.

# The Wheatsheaf
## WINTERBOURNE

HIGH ST., WINTERBOURNE,
AVON. TEL: 0454 773758

## FLEUR DE LYS RESTAURANT

*238 Henleaze Road, Westbury-on-Trym, Bristol.*
*Tel: (0272) 624458*

The Fleur de Lys boasts an experienced chef-proprietor in Gilbert Schneider who has achieved considerable success in both the French and English restaurant trades, and was formerly head chef at the Chester Grosvenor. In the seven years they have been here, Gilbert and his wife, Christine, have created a homely and welcoming restaurant, decorated prettily in peach and Wedgwood blue. The menu divides neatly into French dishes in the evening and English at lunchtime. Recommended starters are seafood platter and pancakes filled with mushrooms, spinach and cream cheese. Of the main courses, your choice may be French duck breast with oyster mushrooms served with a cream sauce or fillet of lamb in puff pastry. Afterwards there are home-made desserts such as crème brûlée and pavlova with fresh blackcurrant sauce.

*Dinner*
*Lunch on Saturday and Sunday – bookings recommended*

*Dinner and luncheon parties (private) by arrangement. No room charge, menus on request.*

*Closed on Monday, Tuesday and Sunday evening*

*À la carte from £17 – £20*
*Sunday lunch £9.50*
*House wine £7.95 per bottle*

*Vegetarian dishes*

*Access, Visa*

### Fleur·de·Lys
#### RESTAURANT

**238 HENLEAZE ROAD, WESTBURY-ON-TRYM, BRISTOL**
Telephone: (0272) 624458

Avon

# FORTE CREST
Bristol

*Filton Road, Hambrook, Bristol.*
*Tel: (0272) 564242; Fax: (0272) 569735*

Situated on the Northern fringes of Bristol, the Forte Crest is contained within 16 acres of landscaped woodlands and lakes. The Pavilion Restaurant is fully air-conditioned, light and spacious. The restaurant, which can seat 170 diners, is arranged to cater for both small and large parties, and offers a delightful view over the landscaped gardens.

The à la carte is innovative without being too long. It offers both vegetarian and diabetic choices, as well as dishes such as terrine of duckling and kumquats, followed by a selection of main courses including fresh lobster from the tank. The range of main courses includes choices to suit all tastes. There is a grill section, and home-made desserts from the trolley conclude.

## The Pavilion Restaurant

Telephone: (0272) 564242

Filton Road,

Hambrook,

Bristol

FORTE CREST
Bristol

Avon

# The PAVILION Restaurant

Candlelit dinner dances are held every Saturday evening, except August, featuring quality dance bands. The traditional family Sunday lunches are still popular and are served in the Pavilion Restaurant, which is open daily for lunch and dinner excluding Saturday lunchtime. For light hot and cold snacks, why not try the Chariots Coffee Shop, open daily from 8am until 9.30pm.

The Pavilion Carvery features a choice of 20 d'oeuvres, plus freshly-made soup. For the main course, there is a choice of two roasts and a variety of entrées, with fresh vegetables, or you can select your own salad from the salad bar.

The Forte Crest offers facilities for conferences and private parties from 5 – 500 people. The 197 bedrooms are all modern and stylish complete with fully equipped *en suite* bathrooms.

*Just off junction 1 of the M32, within easy reach of the M4 and M5*

*Ample car parking for 500 cars*

*Table d'hôte Lunch £14.95*
*Table d'hôte £16.95*
*Light snack meals from £2.95 – £7*
*House wine £8.25*

*Vegetarian and diabetic dishes available*

*Hungry Bear children's menu available*

*A no smoking area*

*Access, Visa, Amex, Diner's Club, Forte Gold Card*

## THE KILN BRASSERIE

*Bristol Hilton International, Redcliffe Way, Bristol.*
*Tel: (0272) 260041*

The Kiln is the last reminder of Bristol's prosperous glass-making industry. Ogen melon with sorbets could be followed by baked chicken and veal roulade. Please see page 13 for more details.

## LE CHATEAU WINE BAR

*32 Park Street, Bristol.*
*Tel: (0272) 268654*

An antique, mirror-backed bar, Victorian snob screen and spiral staircase are all features of this city centre wine bar. Guests could sample fruits de mer, then duck in port and orange sauce, with blueberry pie to conclude. For more information, please see pages 14 and 15.

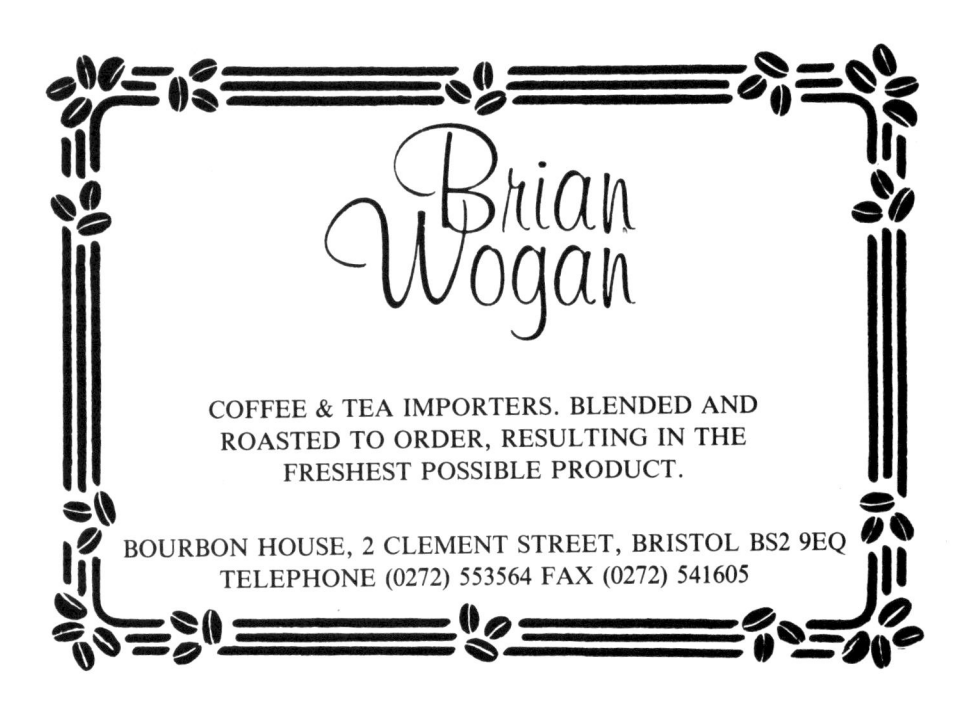

**Brian Wogan**

COFFEE & TEA IMPORTERS. BLENDED AND ROASTED TO ORDER, RESULTING IN THE FRESHEST POSSIBLE PRODUCT.

BOURBON HOUSE, 2 CLEMENT STREET, BRISTOL BS2 9EQ
TELEPHONE (0272) 553564 FAX (0272) 541605

## MICHAELS FASHIONS

*38 Triangle West, Clifton, Bristol.*
*Tel: (0272) 262782*

H ome-made meals and cakes can be found at the restaurant on the first floor of Michaels Fashions. The day starts with English and Continental breakfasts, proceeding through coffees, lunches and cream teas. Jacket potatoes, sandwiches, ploughman's and Danish pastries can all be found here. Private parties are welcome.

*At the top of Park Street, opposite Maples/Gillows*

*Open 9am – 4pm Monday – Friday and 9am – 5pm Saturday*

*Closed all day Sunday*

*Prices between 75p and £4.50*

*Access, Visa, Amex*

**CABOT COFFEE Lounge & Restaurant**

**AT MICHAELS FASHION STORE**
FOR HOME-MADE COOKING & CAKES
38 TRIANGLE WEST, CLIFTON
TEL: (0272) 262782

## RAJDOOT

*83 Park Street, Bristol.*
*Tel: (0272) 268033/291242*

E stablished since 1966, The Rajdoot Group offer authentic North Indian cuisine. Tandoori-style cooking is the speciality of the Bristol Rajdoot, and guests could sample fish tikka and chicken narial. For more information, please see page 16.

## THE UNICORN HOTEL

*Prince Street, Bristol.*
*Tel: (0272) 230333; Fax: (0272) 230300*

S ituated on Narrow Quay, adjoining the city centre, The Unicorn Hotel boasts a Waterfront Tavern offering lunchtime dishes, as well as an 80-seater restaurant. Sample deep-fried Camembert, then sautéd strips of veal in tomato, paprika and yoghurt. Please see page 17 for more information.

Bristol

*Lunch*
*Dinner*

*À la carte £10 – £15*
*House wine £5.95 per bottle*

*Vegetarian dishes*
*Children are welcome*
*Facilities for disabled guests*

*Access, Visa*

## THE GANGES TANDOORI RESTAURANT

*368 Gloucester Road, Bristol.*
*Tel: (0272) 245234*

The décor is opulent and the service attentive at this popular tandoori restaurant. There are many specialities – tandoori machli (marinated fish gently spiced and barbecued) and rezala (a ceremonial dish of lamb). The desserts are for the sweet-toothed – gulab jam is syrup-soaked sponges. There is a take away service.

INDIAN CUISINE — **The Ganges** — INDIAN EXPERIENCE

Enjoy the superb presentation of Tandoori and home-made curry in an elegant and exotic atmosphere with the comfort of air conditioning, maintaining impeccable traditions.
RECOMMENDED BY GOOD FOOD GUIDES
**368 Gloucester Road, Horfield, Bristol. Tel. 245234/428505**

## THE BRISTOL MOAT HOUSE HOTEL

*Victoria Street, Bristol.*
*Tel: (0272) 255010*

The Spires Bar and Restaurant is the setting for international cuisine in this hotel. Sample ravioli of salmon, monkfish and lobster, then filo pastry filled with wild mushrooms. Crème brûlée could conclude. For more information, please see page 18.

## THE BRASS NAILS AT THE GRAND HOTEL

*Broad Street, Bristol.*
*Tel: (0272) 291645; Fax: (0272) 227619*

Mirrored ceilings and walls panelled with Japanese oak set the scene in The Brass Nails. Deep-fried mushrooms stuffed with Stilton and apple could precede Dover sole Albert. There are vegetarian dishes. Please see page 19 for more information.

## HARVEYS RESTAURANT

**12A Denmark Street, Bristol.**
**Tel: (0272) 277665**

The cellars beneath 12 Denmark Street in central Bristol have been in constant use by wine merchants John Harvey & Sons since 1796. As long ago as 1220, records show the same cellars used as part of the Hospital of the Gaunts. Harveys, famous today for sherry, opened the restaurant in the 1960s. Harveys is an Anglo-French establishment and, given the company's 200 years of experience in the wine trade, the wine list boasts a selection ranging from £10 to £840. The list specialises in clarets and vintage ports, dating back to the 1940s and 1920s respectively. On Saturday evenings Harveys Restaurant has a changing programme of live music from local artists. The Harveys Wine Museum (Bristol 277661) is adjacent to the restaurant, and is open in the evenings for visits from guests at the restaurant.

*Centre of Bristol*

*Lunch 12noon – 2.15pm (last orders)*
*Dinner 7 – 11pm (last orders)*

*Closed Saturday lunchtime, all day Sunday and Bank Holidays*

*À la carte £30*
*Table d'hôte luncheon from £14.95*
*House wine from £9.50 per bottle*

*Vegetarian dishes*
*Children's portions*

*Access, Visa, Amex, Diner's Club*

# HARVEYS
## Restaurant

*Combine fine wines with superb food in atmospheric historic cellar surroundings.*

For reservations telephone Bristol (0272) 277665

## THE PARKSIDE HOTEL

*470 Bath Road, Brislington, Bristol.*
*Tel: (0272) 711461*

The Parkside Hotel was built in the mid 1700's by a wealthy merchant, Thomas Reeves. The ornate twin staircase and carved ceilings, uncovered during a recent refurbishment, now form the hotel reception. A walk through to the right leads you into a courtyard hidden in the middle of the building, and the hotel is set in its own grounds amid poplar and spruce trees. The cuisine in the Conservatory Restaurant is varied. Begin with spinach wrapped in filo pastry, or king prawns in garlic butter. Main courses include chicken Madagascar (chicken on a sauce of white wine, green pepper and shallots, finished with cream) and poached salmon with watercress sauce. There are vegetarian dishes such as vegetable lasagne, and sweets can be chosen from the trolley. There is a garden, and weddings and conferences can be accommodated.

*Morning coffee 10am – 12noon*
*Afternoon tea 3 – 5pm*
*Dinner 7 – 10.30pm*
*Bar meals 12noon – 2pm*

*Closed for bar meals Sunday lunchtime*

*À la carte £13*
*Sunday lunch £8.95*
*Bar snacks from £3.15*
*House wine £7.50 per bottle*

*Vegetarian dishes*

*Children's menu*

*Facilities for the disabled*

*Access, Visa, Amex, Diner's Club*

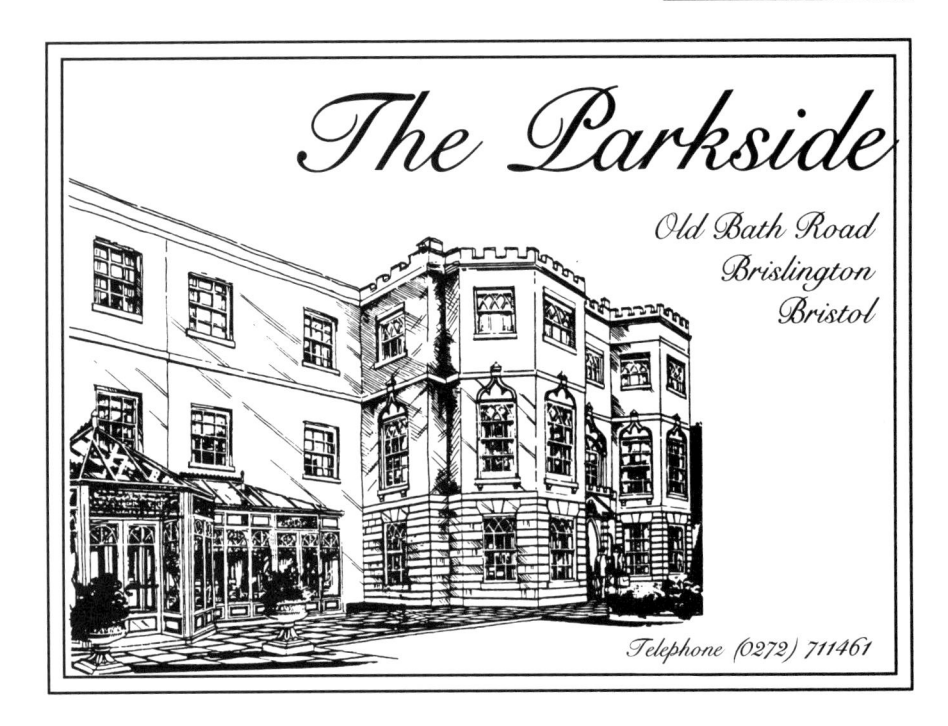

## RESTAURANT DU GOURMET

43 Whiteladies Road, Bristol.
Tel: (0272) 736230; Fax: (0272) 237394

**S**erge and Lucien have been the owners of this highly respected French restaurant for 19 years, during which time its reputation has attracted lovers of authentic French gourmet food. There are covers for 75 guests and a private room for parties of up to 40. There is an extensive à la carte, as well as daily specials. The wine list will please the most discerning connoisseur.

| |
|---|
| On the A4018 |
| Lunch 12noon – 2pm Monday – Friday Dinner 7.15 – 11.15pm Monday – Friday (7.15pm – 12.15am Saturday) |
| Closed Sunday |
| À la carte from £18 House wine from £7.75 per bottle |
| Access, Visa, Amex, Diners |

**RESTAURANT DU**
# GOURMET
Cuisine Française
Fully Licensed

**Proprietors: Serge et Lucien**
**43 Whiteladies Road**
**Bristol BS8 2LS**
**Telephone: 736230**
**Fax: 237394**

## THE CLIFFE HOTEL AND COTERIE RESTAURANT

*Limpley Stoke, near Bath.*
*Tel: (0225) 723226*

**T**he Cliffe Hotel is the domain of Canadians Bill and Tracey Mallinson. French and traditional English cooking forms the backbone of a menu which could feature pan-fried fillet of pork with Oriental vegetables or veal Stroganoff. Please see page 20 for more information.

*'Look out for . . .*
*Where to Eat in*
*Gloucestershire, Oxfordshire & the Cotswolds*
*on sale now!'*

41

## HOWARDS, HOTWELLS
*1A–2A Avon Crescent, Hotwells, Bristol.*
*Tel: (0272) 262921*

*Near the Suspension Bridge and the SS Great Britain*

*Lunch 12noon – 2pm (approx)*
*Dinner 7pm – late*

*Closed for lunch on Saturday and Sunday all day*

*À la carte £15 – £20*
*Table d'hôte set lunch £13*
*Table d'hôte set dinner £15*
*House wine £6.95 per bottle*

*Access, Visa, Amex*

With a view of Bristol's famous Clifton Suspension Bridge from every window, and Brunel's SS Great Britain just around the corner, this Georgian building is fortunate in its interesting and historic waterside position. The long-standing reputation of Chris Howard's restaurant has been built on food, not just the attraction of its location. The Head Chef David Roast has a fresh and exciting approach to food, and he has compiled a quality menu with an often unusual selection of extra dishes from the seasonal blackboard. The presentation is tempting, the atmosphere friendly but efficient, and there are good wines too. Ample waterside car parking is available. The Howards' success has resulted in a new bistro in Nailsea (see below).

## HOWARDS BISTRO
*2 Kings Hill, Nailsea.*
*Tel: (0275) 858348*

*Ten minutes from the city centre*

*Lunch by prior arrangement, except on Sundays when there is a traditional meal*
*Dinner*

*Weekday table d'hôte £9.90 (2 courses)*
*Sunday lunch £7.50 (children's meals available)*

*Regular weekly features with special 3 course menu for £12.50*

*Wednesday wine tasting*

*Friday French evening*

*Access, Visa, Amex*

The Howards have picked an out-of-town location for their new bistro, but it is only ten minutes drive from Bristol's city centre. The pleasant white-washed cottage conversion in Old Nailsea serves sensibly-priced food on its crisp, red-checked tablecloths. The French and traditional menu includes grilled French goat's cheese with basil and pine kernels, then medallions of fillet steak with a port and Stilton sauce.

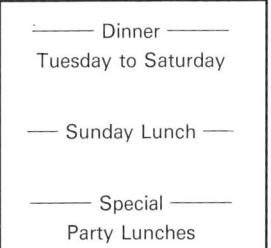

——— Dinner ———
Tuesday to Saturday

——— Sunday Lunch ———

——— Special ———
Party Lunches

**HOWARDS**
B   I   S   T   R   O
Telephone 0275 858348

## THE CHEQUERS INN

*Hanham Mills, Hanham-on-the-River, Bristol.*
*Tel: (0272) 674242*

The Old Chequers Inn used to be the haunt of barge men, who drank rough ales and cider from pewter pots. The inn was once involved in the Duke of Monmouth's Protestant uprising against King James, and Conan Doyle's novel *Micah Clark* describes how the Duke's rebel army was drawn up alongside The Chequers whilst the King's army was on the other side of the river. The current inn was built nearly 100 years ago, and the Roasters Bar carvery provides wholesome home cooking. A possible meal could be deep-fried mushrooms, followed by beef Stroganoff, or smoked salmon then lasagne. Cheesecake, chocolate fudge cake and banana split are amongst the desserts. Sundays see traditional roast beef and Yorkshire pudding on the menu.

*On the River Avon, midway between Bristol and Bath*

*Lunch 12noon – 2.30pm*
*Dinner 7 – 11pm*
*Bar meals 12noon – 2.30pm and 6 – 10pm*

*À la carte £10*
*Sunday lunch £6.95*
*Bar meals from £2.50*
*House wine £6.50 per bottle; £1.30 per glass*

*Vegetarian dishes*

*Children catered for*

*Access, Visa, Amex*

# The Chequers Inn
Hanham-on-the-River, Bristol. Telephone (0272) 674242

## THE RIVERSIDE RESTAURANT AT SALTFORD MARINA

*The Shallows, Saltford, near Bath.*
*Tel: (0225) 873862*

The Riverside Restaurant overlooks the River Avon at Kelston Lock. There are chef's specials in addition to the à la carte which may feature Caribbean chicken, beef Stroganoff or vegetarian envelope. There is a carvery at Sunday lunchtime. Please see page 21 for more information.

## THE CANARY SHOP AND RESTAURANT

*3 Queen Street, Bath.*
*Tel: (0225) 424846*

A selection of over 40 fine teas has resulted in The Canary being voted the Top Tea Room of the Year by the Tea Council in past years. However Continental and English breakfasts can also be sampled here, along with lunch and supper. Please see page 22 for more information.

---

*Centre of Bath*

Lunch 12 noon – 2.30pm
Dinner 6 – 11.30pm

À la carte £10 – £14
House wine £5.95 per bottle

Vegetarian dishes

Access, Visa

## BENGAL BRASSERIE

*32 Milsom Street, Bath.*
*Tel: (0225) 447906*

A pleasant rendezvous for a romantic dinner, Bengal Brasserie offers intimate alcoves with hanging lanterns, but just as readily welcomes larger groups. The menu, based on Indian provincial cooking, has all the classics: tikka, tandoori, vindaloo and vegetarian. There are set menus too, and a business lunch option. A 10% discount is offered on the efficient and quick take aways.

---

**Bengal Brasserie**
32, Milsom Street, Bath, Avon
Tel: (0225) 447906

**Specialists in Tandoori and Curries**

Open Daily: 12 Noon – 2.30pm
6.00pm – 11.30pm
Including Holidays
Specially Prepared Lunch
Mon – Fri: 12.00 – 2.00pm
Fully Air Conditioned
Take Away

## ÉDOUARD'S WINE BAR, RESTAURANT AND POISSONERIE

*31 Belvedere, Lansdown Road, Bath.*
*Tel: (0225) 333042*

This attractive 300-year-old building on three levels houses a wine bar with restaurant; a relaxed cellar lounge bar, with doors opening onto a delightful garden; and, on the upper floor, a spacious baronial hall, complete with minstrel's gallery and separate bar with dining area, all tastefully decorated in tones of oyster-grey and hung with pictures by original artists. Many of the pictures echo the connections with the sea emphasised on the menu which operates on all floors, fresh seafood coming from Brixham, Devon. From the varied selection of dishes a choice could include a warm salad of crispy duck with a Grand Marnier dressing, or a warm salad of sautéd scallops and lardons with garlic and herbs, to start. Monkfish sautéd in butter, served with a lobster sauce, or escalope of veal with a Stilton and cream sauce, may then be followed by sherry soufflé with a Maraschino cherry sauce.

*Centre of Bath*
*Morning coffee*
*Lunch*
*Dinner*

*Closed Bank Holidays*

*À la carte £11*
*Bar snacks from £1.95 – £5*
*House wine £6.85 per bottle*

*Access, Visa*

---

## Édouard's
### Wine Bar
### Restaurant & Poissonerie

Open Monday to Sunday

**31 Belvedere, Lansdown Rd**

For reservations phone
**Bath (0225) 333042**

## NUMBER 1 RESTAURANT AT THE COMPASS HOTEL

*North Parade, Bath.*
*Tel: (0225) 461603; Fax: (0225) 447758*

S ituated in the heart of Bath, The Compass Hotel reopened in 1990 after extensive refurbishment. Beef sate is a possible starter, before Bath rib roast. Chocolate and Cointreau bavarois is a tempting dessert. Please see page 23 for more information.

## SALLY LUNN'S REFRESHMENT HOUSE

*4 North Parade Passage, Bath.*
*Tel: (0225) 461634*

N amed after the famous Sally Lunn brioche, this old eating house offers guests set menus in the evening that are good value for money. Wines are sold at the same cost per bottle, plus wholesale price, therefore some real bargains are to be found here. For more information, please see page 24.

## THE THEATRE VAULTS RESTAURANT

*The Theatre Royal, Bath.*
*Tel: (0225) 442265*

T he original vaults of the Georgian Theatre Royal are the unusual setting for this restaurant serving French-influenced cuisine. The daily changed menus could feature croque madame, chicken liver crêpe, pork cassoulet or spinach lasagne. For more information, please see page 25.

## THE ROYAL CRESCENT HOTEL

*16 Royal Crescent, Bath.*
*Tel: (0225) 319090; Fax: (0225) 339401*

B ath's famous Royal Crescent is home to the elegant Royal Crescent Hotel, and the Dower House Restaurant mixes classical décor with fine paintings and real fires. Once the home of the Lady Dowager, English cuisine now features here, such as lasagne of langoustines in a soft herb butter and chicken marinated with oriental spices. Please see page 26 for more information.

## HUNTSMAN INN

*North Parade, Bath.*
*Tel: (0225) 460100/428812;*
*Fax: (0225) 480866*

**B**ath, of course, is a city characterised by its elegant buildings of Georgian stone, and The Huntsman now has the oldest surviving stone shop front in the city, with, behind it, a popular pub and restaurant. The Cellar Bar is flagstoned and has an interesting collection of old bottles from its days as a bottling plant for the brewers Eldridge Pope and Co. Today the bar serves a menu covering the whole range of pub sandwiches and ploughman's lunches. On the first floor is a restaurant dating back to the 15th century when it was used by monks for accommodation. From the menu come roast meats, home-made pies, grills, salads and fish. Typical of the choice is steak and kidney pudding with Guinness and mushrooms, salmon steak au gratin with a lemon and cucumber sauce and sauté of chicken with a Burgundy sauce.

*Centre of Bath*

*Morning coffee*
*Lunch*
*Afternoon tea*
*Dinner*
*Bar meals all day.*

*À la carte £8.50*
*Sunday lunch £7.50*
*Bar snacks from £1.20*
*House wine from £8.40 per carafe; £4.40 per half carafe*

*Vegetarian dishes*
*Children's menu*

## Huntsman Inn, Bath

(Over 250 Years Old)

*Cellar Bar with genuine flagstone floor – and Royal Oak the tradtiional ale from the Hardy Country Delicious home-made food served in the bar orin the historic restaurant upstairs Banqueting facilities for approximately 100 persons. Weddings, Dinners, Dinner Dances etc, Conferences.*

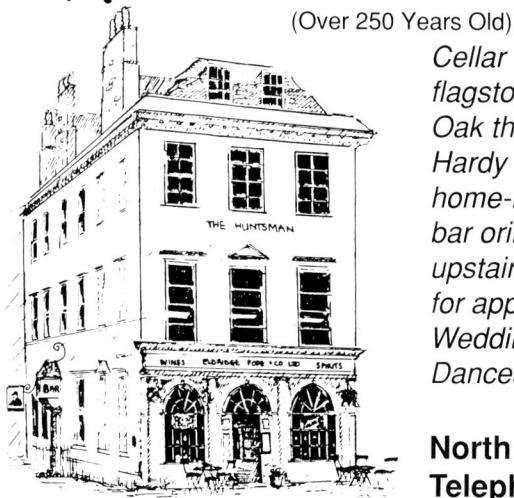

*Open All Day*

**North Parade, Bath**
**Telephone 460100**
**Fax 0225 480866**

Bath

*Near the Royal Crescent*

*Morning coffee 10.30 – 12noon*
*Lunch 12noon – 2pm*
*Afternoon tea (in summer) 3 – 5pm*
*Dinner 7 – 10.30pm*

*À la carte £10*
*Bar meals from £2.50*
*House wine from £6.90*

*Vegetarian dishes*

*Children catered for*

*Access, Visa*

## VENDANGE WINE BAR

*11 Margarets Buildings, Brock Street, Bath.*
*Tel: (0225) 421251*

This wine bar offers a warm, friendly, relaxed atmosphere and has umbrellas outside in a traffic-free precinct. Good taste has been shown in the redecoration and a nice touch are the fresh flowers on each table. Hostess is Shaw Hardisty, a lady who quite obviously enjoys her work in creating Continental and traditional meals from fresh ingredients. Pâtés, ratatouille with garlic bread, chicken baked in cream and courgettes, aubergine croustade and tagliatelle with garlic mushrooms and tomato sauce – all feature from time to time. Special puddings include chocolate St Emilion, gâteaux, fruit pies and sorbets, and popular wines are on the list to ensure that meals have the right accompaniment. Daily specials appear on a blackboard, there is occasional live music and a garden for summer dining.

We offer good food, wine, beer, spirits, coffee in a friendly atmosphere at reasonable prices.

Our home-cooked food is wholesome and delicious.

**Vendange WINE BAR**

11 Margarets Buildings, Bath BA1 2LP
Tel. (0225) 421251

## PASTA GALORE

*31 Barton Street, Bath.*
*Tel: (0225) 463861*

Now in its sixth year, this authentic Italian restaurant is as popular as ever. Charmingly decorated, it seats 45, and there is extra seating in the garden. Sample prosciutto e melone, then spaghetti con gamberi capricciosa. There is also a daily blackboard special.

*Near the Theatre Royal*

*Lunch 12noon – 2.30pm*
*Dinner 6 – 10.30pm Mon-Wed; 6 – 11pm Thurs – Sat*

*Closed Sundays*

*À la carte £10 (3 courses)*
*House wine £6.40 per bottle*

*Vegetarian dishes*

*Access, Visa*

**PASTA GALORE**
RISTORANTE
31 Barton Street, Bath. Tel (0225) 463861
Shops: 4 Broad St. Bath Tel 464060
16 The Berkley Centre 15-19 Queens Road Bristol Tel 273184

## THE LANSDOWN GROVE HOTEL

*Lansdown Road, Bath.*
*Tel: (0225) 315891*

This elegant hotel overlooks the city of Bath, and affords all visitors a gracious welcome. Warm salad of smoked chicken and asparagus is a possible starter, and could be followed by fricassée of Cornish scallops. The cheeseboard could conclude. Please see page 27 for more information.

## THE WATER WHEEL RESTAURANT

*Old Mill Hotel, Tollbridge Road, Bath.*
*Tel: (0225) 858476; Fax: (0225) 852600*

The Old Mill, as its name suggests, enjoys an idyllic setting astride the River Avon. The Mill Room is available for bar meals, whilst more formal dining is available in the revolving Water Wheel Restaurant. Please see page 28 for more information.

Bath

*Centre of Bath*

Lunch 12noon – 2pm
Dinner 6 – 11pm (last orders)

À la carte £18
House wine £7 per bottle

Access, Visa, Amex, Diner's Club

## RAJPOOT TANDOORI

*4 Argyle Street, Bath.*
*Tel: (0225) 466833/464758*

Stone arches divide the Rajpoot into three sections, each with its own individual character. It is always advisable to book, and the restaurant has received many recommendations. Its specialities include tandooris and dishes such as chicken Jaflang (a curry-type dish using special herbs and spices collected from the hills of Jaflang). There is a large wine list.

An authentic fayre for the connoisseur of good food. has an established reputation for serving its own blend of subtle Tandoori and Curry dishes, all prepared with a great skill and attention to detail.

*Internationally renowned and highly recommended by good food guides. Fully air conditioned.*
Open Daily 12 noon – 2.30pm   6pm – 11pm Last orders

**Europe's most exclusive Raj cuisine in an elegant and exotic atmosphere.**

RAJPOOT HOUSE, 4 ARGYLE STREET, BATH. TEL: 466833/464758. FAX: 0225 442462

---

Dinner
Sunday lunch

À la carte £20
Sunday lunch £9.50
Bar snacks £1.50
House wine

Access, Visa

## BENTLEY'S RESTAURANT AT THE REDCAR HOTEL

*Henrietta Street, Bath.*
*Tel: (0225) 469151*

The Redcar Hotel is a smart Georgian conversion, distinguished by Bath stonewalling. Its restaurant, Bentley's, is decorated in beige and caters for a wide-ranging clientele that includes both family and business diners. There is a chef's choice menu of the day on offer, and a seasonally changing à la carte selection.

BENTLEY'S RESTAURANT

at the Redcar Hotel
Henrietta Street
Bath
BA2 6LR

Tel (0225) 469151

50

## CHOPSTICK

*33 Southgate, Bath.*
*Tel: (0225) 425067*

This small, cosy Chinese restaurant is conveniently situated in the middle of Bath. Owner Mr Wong has been in residence 21 years and he makes up a successful team with his uncle who is the chef. Popular starters include hot and sour soup and salt and pepper rib, while for main course there is roast duck, diced chicken in hot chilli sauce, quick-fried squid, or shredded beef. Banana fritters are tempting, or for something refreshing to finish the meal, there are lychees. The house wine is French but there are Chinese wines too. The names are full of promise – Great Wall, Harmony, Dynasty. Take aways are available, but it seems a shame to miss out on the charming character of this popular restaurant, with its welcoming Chinese lantern an attractive focal point in the centre of the dining area. Parties are happily catered for.

*Centre of Bath*

Lunch 12noon – 2pm
Dinner 5.30 – 11.30pm
Sunday 12noon – 11.30pm

À la carte £6
Table d'hôte £8.50
House wine £4.95 per bottle

*Vegetarian dishes*
*Children's portions*

*Access, Visa*

---

## Chopstick
### Chinese Restaurant and Take Away
**33 SOUTHGATE, BATH. TELEPHONE 425067**

FULLY LICENSED

AIR CONDITIONED

Three Course Business Lunch, Monday – Saturday
Open daily 12 noon–2.00 pm, 5.30 pm–11.30 pm
Sunday 12 noon–11.30 pm
Cantonese Cuisine
Special Parties Catered For.

## NIGHTINGALES

*The Bridge, Lower Limpley Stoke, Bath.*
*Tel: (0225) 723150*

This old stone boathouse, now a restaurant, has been refurbished by new owners, Andrea and Mary Colla, with a warm pink décor and candlelit tables laid with fresh linen and white china. The menu offers regional Italian cuisine, leaving the full range of Italian dishes for special gourmet evenings. The standard menu is interestingly conceived and employs both simple and complicated ideas. For a light lunch, try smoked salmon, followed by baked halibut with white wine and herb sauce. A more substantial meal might appeal: pancakes filled with three kinds of cheese and served on a tomato and basil sauce, then escalope of salmon in white wine sauce, followed by shin of veal with mixed vegetable and saffron rice. The vegetarian choice includes avocado, mozzarella and tomato on an olive oil and basil dressing.

---

*Lunch by appointment only*
*Dinner 7 – 10.30pm (last orders 10pm)*

*Closed Sunday afternoon and all day Monday*

À la carte (3 course) £15.75
À la carte (2 course) £13.25
Sunday lunch £8.50
House wine £5.95 per bottle

*Vegetarian dishes are available*

*Access, Visa*

---

**Nightingales**

OPENING HOURS
Tues – Sat 7pm – 10.30pm
Sunday 12.30pm – 2.00pm

Nightingales
The Bridge
Lower Limpley Stoke
Bath, Avon
Tel: (0225) 723150

## THE PORTCULLIS INN

High Street, Tormarton, Badminton.
Tel: (045 4218) 263

The village of Tormarton nestles into the Cotswolds on the Wilts/Avon/Gloucestershire border, and is easily reached from the M4. The menu offers a range of home-cooked meals at reasonable prices. As a free house, The Portcullis also prides itself on a wide choice of real ales, and accommodation is provided in seven rooms.

$^{1}/_{2}$ mile from Junction 18 of the M4

Morning coffee
Lunch
Dinner

Sunday lunch £6.90
Bar snacks from £1.60
House wine £5.25 per bottle

Vegetarian dishes

Children welcomed
Facilities for disabled guests

Accommodation – 7 **en suite** rooms; £35 double, £30 single
Rates include full breakfast
Special weekend rate

Access, Visa

## LUCKNAM PARK

Colerne.
Tel: (0225) 742777; Fax: (0225) 743536

Lucknam Park is a Georgian country house, set just six miles outside Bath. Modern English cuisine is the order of the day, with starters such as tagliatelli with pesto sauce and cherry tomatoes, followed by salmis of squab pigeon with a parsley sauce. Please see page 29 for more details.

Whilst we believe all details are correct, we suggest that readers check, when making reservations, that prices and other facts quoted meet with their requirements.

## THE FOUNTAIN INN & BOXERS RESTAURANT

*1 St Thomas Street, Wells.*
*Tel: (0749) 672317*

The Fountain was built during the 16th century to house builders working on the famous cathedral nearby. The inn's bar is panelled and hung with pictures of local interest, whilst Boxers Restaurant has Laura Ashley décor of pine and chintz. Both the restaurant and the bar serve the same menu, the only difference being the waitress service in the former. Begin with moules marinière, or warm chicken and bacon salad. Lamb valentine (with a redcurrant and rosemary sauce), game in season and fresh fish are available as main courses. For dessert there are home-made strudels and fruit pies. Owners Sarah and Adrian Lawrence have won a *Les Routiers* award for their selection of West Country cheeses.

*On the A34, on the outskirts of Wells*

*Morning coffee 10.30am – 12noon*
*Lunch 11.30am – 2pm Mon – Sat; 12noon – 2pm (last orders) Sun*
*Dinner 6 – 10pm Mon – Sat; 7 – 9.30pm Sun*
*Bar meals as above*

*Restaurant closed lunchtimes except Sunday*

*À la carte £12.50*
*Bar snacks from £1 – £9.50*
*House wine £5.95 per bottle*

*Vegetarian dishes*
*Children catered for*
*Gourmet evenings hosted*

*Access, Visa, Amex*

---

*The Fountain Inn & Boxers Restaurant*

### Food, Glorious Food

*1 St. Thomas Street,*
*Wells, Somerset*
*Tel: Wells (0749) 672317*

Recommended by Egon Ronay, Les Routiers, the Somerset Good Food Guide and Consumers Association – 'Out to Eat' Guide.

Famished in Felixstowe?
Hungry in Holyhead?
Peckish in Perth?
Ravenous in Roscommon?

# WHERE TO EAT

The discerning diner's guide to restaurants throughout Britain and Ireland

WHERE TO EAT IN SURREY
WHERE TO EAT IN GLOUCESTERSHIRE OXFORDSHIRE & THE COTSWOLDS
WHERE TO EAT IN IRELAND
WHERE TO EAT IN THAMES & CHILTERNS BERKS · HERTS · BUCKS · BEDS
WHERE TO EAT IN KENT
WHERE TO EAT IN IRELAND
WHERE TO EAT IN SUSSEX
WHERE TO EAT IN KENT
WHERE TO EAT IN SCOTLAND
WHERE TO EAT IN DORSET & SOUTH WILTSHIRE
WHERE TO EAT IN SUSSEX
WHERE TO EAT IN BRISTOL · BATH · AVON SOMERSET & WILTSHIRE

*Copies available from bookshops or direct from the publishers*
**Kingsclere Publications Ltd**
*Use the Order Form On Page 56*

# ORDER FORM

To:
**KINGSCLERE PUBLICATIONS LTD.**
Highfield House, 2 Highfield Avenue, Newbury, Berkshire RG14 5DS

Please send me

| | |
|---|---|
| ____copies of *WHERE TO EAT* in **BRISTOL, BATH, AVON** at £2.50 | £____ |
| ____copies of *WHERE TO EAT* in **BERKSHIRE** at £1.95 | £____ |
| ____copies of *WHERE TO EAT* in the **CHANNEL ISLANDS** at £1.25 | £____ |
| ____copies of *WHERE TO EAT* in **CORNWALL** at £2.50 | £____ |
| ____copies of *WHERE TO EAT* in **CUMBRIA & NORTH WEST ENGLAND** at £2.50 | £____ |
| ____copies of *WHERE TO EAT* in **DORSET & SOUTH WILTSHIRE** at £2.95 | £____ |
| ____copies of *WHERE TO EAT* in **EAST ANGLIA & ESSEX** at £2.50 | £____ |
| ____copies of *WHERE TO EAT* in **EAST MIDLANDS** at £1.95 | £____ |
| ____copies of *WHERE TO EAT* in **GLOUCESTERSHIRE, OXFORDSHIRE & THE COTSWOLDS** at £2.50 | £____ |
| ____copies of *WHERE TO EAT* in **HAMPSHIRE & WILTSHIRE** at £2.50 | £____ |
| ____copies of *WHERE TO EAT* in **IRELAND** at £3.50 | £____ |
| ____copies of *WHERE TO EAT* in **KENT** at £2.50 | £____ |
| ____copies of *WHERE TO EAT* in **NORTH EAST ENGLAND** at £1.95 | £____ |
| ____copies of *WHERE TO EAT* in **SCOTLAND** at £2.95 | £____ |
| ____copies of *WHERE TO EAT* in **SURREY** at £2.50 | £____ |
| ____copies of *WHERE TO EAT* in **SUSSEX** at £2.50 | £____ |
| ____copies of *WHERE TO EAT* in **THAMES & CHILTERNS** at £2.50 | £____ |
| ____copies of *WHERE TO EAT* in **WALES** at £3.50 | £____ |
| ____copies of *WHERE TO EAT* in **YORKSHIRE & HUMBERSIDE** at £2.50 | £____ |

p&p at £0.50 (single copy), £1 (2-5 copies), £2 (6 copies)

**GRAND TOTAL** £____

Name ........................................................
Address .....................................................
............................................................
Postcode ........................... Cheque enclosed £..............

Your help in answering the following would be appreciated:

(1) Did you buy this guide at a SHOP ❑ TOURIST OFFICE ❑ GARAGE ❑ OTHER ❑

(2) Are any of your favourite eating places *not* listed in this guide? If so, could you please supply names and locations ..........................
............................................................
............................................................

# IF AN ADVERT IS IN PRINT, IS IT PROPER?

Most advertisements are perfectly proper.
A few are not.

The Advertising Standards Authority not only monitors over 850 advertisements every month, it ensures compliance with the rules in the strict Code of Advertising Practice.

So when you question an advertiser, they have to answer to us.

To find out more about the role of the ASA, please write to the address below.

Advertising Standards Authority, Department X, Brook House, Torrington Place, London WC1E 7HN.

**ASA**

**This space is donated in the interests of high standards in advertisements.**

# INDEX

## ALPHABETICAL INDEX TO ESTABLISHMENTS

Bengal Brasserie, Bath..................................................................................44
Bentley's Restaurant at the Redcar Hotel, Bath............................................50
The Bowl Inn & Restaurant, Lower Almondsbury.........................................31
The Brass Nails at the Grand Hotel, Bristol..................................................19
Brian Wogan, Bristol.....................................................................................36
The Bristol Moat House Hotel, Bristol..........................................................18
The Canary Shop and Restaurant, Bath........................................................22
Le Chateau Wine Bar, Bristol........................................................................14
The Chequers Inn, Hanham-on-the-River, Bristol........................................43
Chopstick, Bath.............................................................................................51
The Cliffe Hotel and Coterie Retaurant, Limpley Stoke, near Bath.............20
Edouard's Wine Bar, Restaurant and Poissonerie, Bath...............................45
Fleur de Lys Restaurant, Westbury-on-Trym, Bristol....................................33
The Fountain Inn & Boxers Restaurant, Wells..............................................54
The Forte Crest Hotel, Hambrook, Bristol....................................................34
The Ganges Tandoori Restaurant, Bristol.....................................................38
The Grange Resort Hotel, Northwood, Winterbourne..................................12
Harvey Restaurant, Bristol............................................................................39
Howards Bistro, Nailsea................................................................................42
Howard, Hotwells, Bristol.............................................................................42
Huntsman Inn, Bath......................................................................................47
The Kiln Brasserie, Bristol Hilton International, Bristol..............................13
The Kitchen Garden, Old Down House, Tockington....................................11
Lansdown Grove Hotel, Bath........................................................................27
Lucknam Park, Colerne................................................................................29
Michaels Fashions, Bristol............................................................................37
Nightingales, Lower Limpley Stoke, Bath....................................................52
Number One Restaurant at the Compass Hotel, Bath..................................23
The Parkside Hotel, Brislington, Bristol.......................................................40
Pasta Galore, Bath........................................................................................49
The Portcullis Inn, Tormarton, Bristol..........................................................53
Rajdoot, Bristol.............................................................................................16
Rajpoot Tandoori, Bath.................................................................................50
Redwood Lodge Hotel & Country Club, Failand, Bristol...............................9
Restaurant du Gourmet, Bristol....................................................................41
The Riverside Restaurant at Saltford Marina, Saltford, near Bath...............21
The Royal Crescent Hotel, Bath....................................................................26
Sally Lunn's Refreshment House, Bath.........................................................24

The Theatre Vaults Restaurant, The Theatre Royal, Bath............................. 25
Thornbury Castle, Thornbury, near Bristol..................................................... 10
Unicorn Hotel, Bristol...................................................................................... 17
Vendange Wine Bar, Bath................................................................................ 48
The Water Wheel Restaurant, The Old Mill Hotel, Bath............................. 28
The Wheatsheaf, Winterbourne...................................................................... 32

## ALPHABETICAL INDEX TO TOWNS AND VILLAGES

| | |
|---|---|
| Bath | 22,44 |
| Brislington | 40 |
| Bristol | 13,36 |
| Colerne | 29 |
| Failand | 9 |
| Hambrook | 34 |
| Hanham-on-the-River | 43 |
| Hotwells | 42 |
| Limpley Stoke | 20 |
| Lower Almondsbury | 31 |
| Lower Limpley Stoke | 52 |
| Nailsea | 42 |
| Saltford | 21 |
| Thornbury | 10 |
| Tockington | 11 |
| Tormarton | 53 |
| Wells | 54 |
| Westbury-on-Trym | 33 |
| Winterbourne | 12,32 |